Soups, Salads,
Memories
of
Milo

There is nothing more heart warming
than a nice hot pot
of soup simmering on the kitchen stove
on a cold winter's day.
Just the satisfaction
of putting it all
together and watching the end result of
a wonderful
soup emerge make the time spent well
worth it.

Soups, Salads, Memories of Milo

Kathryn Renée Vaclav

Illustrations by

Debra L. Heabel

Copyright 1997 by Milo Industries

Illustrations 1997 by Debra L. Heabel

Printed and Bound in the United States of America.

Library of Congress Catalog Number: 97-93618

ISBN: 0-9656522-0-3

Milo Industries, P. O. Box 103, 80 Burr Ridge Parkway, Burr Ridge, Illinois 60521

To my husband Tim, who never let me
say, "I give up", and to
Bonnie Mickelson, who made me
believe I could,
and, of course, to Milo, who will always
be with me in spirit.

Acknowledgments

A special thank-you to my husband Tim, who made me believe in myself and would not let me give up a dream and a memory.

To Bonnie Mickelson, who became a special friend the first time we met. Without her belief and help this book would not have been possible.

To my cousin Debbie, who brought Milo back to life in her drawings.

To the Burr Ridge Veterinary Clinic, who went above and beyond to give Tim and me that extra special time with our beloved Milo.

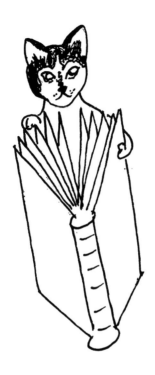

Contents

What's Inside for Salads 90

What's Inside for a Few Extras 118

Milo Stories

About Milo

This book is about Milo. The stories herein are everyday occurrences with Milo that made each day a treasure in our hearts.

Milo is no longer with us. Milo died of a feline blood disease for which there is no cure. Once it was diagnosed, you may have only a few hours with your beloved friend or a more fortunate few months. Milo fought to survive for an incredible eight months. We were so blessed.

Milo died where he was most happy, at home and in our arms. He gave it his all. He endured endless blood transfusions only to come home to start all over again. I know in my heart that his spirit never gave up; unfortunately, his body finally did.

During Milo's illness he showed me what courage, determination, compassion, and love really are. I saw more strength in Milo than I have ever seen in a human being. He fought to the very end to be with us to enjoy the things that we had always enjoyed together. That's why this cookbook was written. Without Milo, it would not have been possible. It is so easy in life to give up, to not accomplish things that you want so much to do or achieve. Well, with the determination that Milo had to the very end, I learned that anything is possible.

This book is not fancy, and the recipes are not difficult or time consuming (I learned from Milo that time is very precious). It just represents what we shared together; I love to cook and he loved to participate and supervise.

And so lives on his special memory throughout these pages. Milo gave us three very short years, but those years will last a lifetime in our hearts.

Everyone, at some point in time, has some event or some person that touches her for the rest of her life. For me, it was Milo, a furry, black and white ball, who came into our lives so unexpectedly. Here is Milo's story and the reason this book came to be.

One chilly October afternoon, while on a family outing in a nearby forest preserve, my husband, Tim, and his two young sons came upon a towel-covered cage. In it were a bunch of mewing kittens, maybe as many as a dozen. (To this day, I shutter to think why they might have been hidden there.) In curiosity, one of the boys opened the cage door, and out they tumbled, scattering in different directions. They quickly disappeared into the woods; all except a little female, who remained cowering and crying, and a black and white male, who seemed to gallantly stay behind to protect his sister (and I truly believe that!).

And so Milo and Millie came home with us, so tiny that they fit into the palms of our hands. Our intentions were to keep them just for the night, giving them a much-needed meal and a warm bed before taking them to the shelter the next day. We lived in a small apartment with an 18-year old cat named Kelly. There just didn't seem to be enough room for 2 more.

Well days turned into weeks, and then into months. We just could not part with our new friends. So we found a nice home in the suburbs, with a wonderful yard for a garden, and thus the adventure began.

Milo and Millie combed every inch of our new home. To Milo it was the greatest and biggest toy he had ever had. There was so much to explore and so many places to hide, when an ambush was necessary. Milo soon became head of the household. He realized he could jump from the floor to the top of the china cabinet with ease. Of course we held our breath each time he tried it. And there he would stay, basking in the sun and watching the birds and the trees move with the wind. Milo found joy in everything he encountered. A dust speck became a rival enemy that had to be taken care of. A spider? Well that was another story. He would keep close guard then kindly escort it out of sight. A bell on the fireplace that for some unforeseen reason he felt he had to ring each day. All was a wonder to him. He could just not get enough of our new home.

Then it was time for the garden. Milo was never let outside but oh when I brought in all the wonderful vegetables from the garden he would just go nuts. Green beans; I'm still finding them hidden under furniture and places you would not believe. Tomatoes; red balls planted just for Milo to play with. Peas; little green bugs to chase. Everything we planted in the garden Milo instantly took possession of.

He would watch in the window so intently as I gathered vegetables from the garden and then place them all on the kitchen counter. Not exactly knowing what I was up to, he would sit patiently waiting for my next move. When I began cooking, Milo began supervising. He would jump on the counter and inspect everything.

Who knows what he was looking for. It seemed everything needed to be inspected before it went into the pot. And if by chance I was not paying him much attention, that little paw would come out and give me a whack as if to say, "Hey, don't forget I'm here".

Milo never let me cook alone. He would lie on the counter until I was done. I would end up with pieces of carrots, celery, beans, peas, onions, you name it, all over the place. I could have cut my cooking time in half if I had not had to retrieve all the contents from various places in the house. It must have been quite a sight though, me chasing a cat running through the house with a green bean dangling from his mouth.

It was really comforting to have Milo's company. I would talk to him and explain what I was making and of course sharing what I could with him. He was the greatest critic, he never told me what was wrong with the dishes, then again he never told me what was right, either. Maybe this is why I really enjoy cooking. Having Milo's company while I was creating made the time so enjoyable. He was my assistant, my inspector, my supervisor, my critic and, of course, my best friend. Cooking became a pastime that I loved, and I know Milo loved it too. He seemed to look forward to not the eating but the preparing of everything. I like to think that Milo found that time with me special also.

What's Cooking in Soups

Split Pea Soup
Sausage and Potato Soup
Tim's Thanksgiving Soup
Black-eyed Pea Soup
White Bean and Sausage Soup
Dill Pickle Soup
Lima Bean Soup
Old Fashioned Beef Dumpling Soup
Cream of Tomato Soup
Yellow Split Pea and Meatball Soup
Hamburger Soup
Grandma's Chicken Soup
Tim's Chicken Soup and Chicken Dinner
Mary's Baked French Onion Soup
Sauerkraut Soup
Beef Barley Soup
Lentil Soup
Cream of Vegetable Soup
Cream of Potato Soup
Fresh Chunky Tomato Soup

Split Pea Soup

The hardest part about this soup is finding a nice ham bone. If you don't have a ham bone use a smoked ham hock. Just as tasty and a little smokier. This soup creates itself, you can't go wrong. I like the vegetables minced very fine, which seems to make it creamier.

Ingredients you will need

2 Tablespoons of Butter
1 Tablespoon of Olive Oil
2 Carrots - Finely Minced
1 Medium Onion - Finely Minced
2 Celery Stalks - Finely Minced
1 Clove of Garlic - Finely Minced
1 Ham Bone or Ham Hock
1 Bag of Green Split Peas
1 Potato - Diced
2 Quarts of Water
1/2 Teaspoon of Black Pepper
1 Bay Leaf

How to Create Your Soup

Sauté in the butter and olive oil the carrots, onion, celery and garlic for approximately ten minutes. Add the ham bone or ham hock, split peas, potato, 1/2 teaspoon of pepper, bay leaf and water. Bring to a full boil and then turn down and simmer about 1 to 1 1/2 hours. When done take the meat from the bones and return to the pot.

That's it!

I love this soup with just a touch of wine vinegar in it.

Serve with warm garlic bagel chips on the side.

Thoughts, memories, recipes and notes:

_____

_____

_____

_____

_____

_____

_____

_____

_____

_____

_____

_____

_____

_____

_____

_____

_____

_____

_____

_____

_____

Ben Gay

Milo never paid much attention when I was making this soup. I guess because I wouldn't be in the kitchen long enough to spark his interest.

One time he grabbed a raw split pea and took off, only to be found seconds later with the pea next to him and a look on his face that if he could talk would have said, "What in the world is that?" After that he was not at all interested in split peas. However he would try anything once then make his decision as to whether he liked it or not. He would try anything from dill pickles, which by the way he loved, to Ben Gay, which by the way he hated. His curiosity got him one time. I had put Ben Gay on and he was so interested he just had to try it. Immediately the eyes started running, he started sneezing and drooling. Then gave me a look that it was all my fault. After that if he even smelled something similar to Ben Gay, he would turn tail and run.

Sausage and Potato Soup

This soup is so thick and rich. It's wonderful on a chilly winter's night. Serve with a nice loaf of fresh baked bread and enjoy!

Ingredients you will need

2 Tablespoons of Olive Oil
1 Tablespoon of Butter
1 Large Clove of Garlic - Minced
3 Green Onions - Sliced
1 Stalk of Celery - Sliced
1 Carrot - Sliced
1 Small White Onion - Diced
2 Tablespoons Chopped Fresh Parsley
1/2 Pound Smoked Polish Sausage (sliced)
1 Parsnip - Diced
3 Medium Potatoes - Diced
2 Quarts of Water
1/4 Teaspoon of Dill Weed
1/8 Teaspoon of Chili Powder
1/4 Teaspoon of White Pepper
1/2 Teaspoon of Salt
1/4 Teaspoon of Basil
1 Tablespoon of Flour
1 Cup of Sour Cream

How to Create Your Soup

In soup pot sauté in olive oil and butter the garlic, green onions, celery, carrot and onion until transparent. Add fresh parsley, Polish sausage, parsnips, potatoes and water. Stir all together well. Add the dill weed, chili powder, white pepper, salt and basil. Bring to a full boil. Boil 15 minutes and then turn down and simmer about an hour or until the soup has started to thicken.

Stir 1 tablespoon of flour in the 1 cup of sour cream and blend well. Add some hot broth to the sour cream mixture and whisk until well blended. Add this to the soup pot. Stir well with a whisk and barely simmer about 15 minutes.

Try not to boil.

Warm Floor

In Tim's apartment there was a spot on the floor that was always toasty warm. We couldn't keep anything there because of the heat. That seemed to be just fine with the kittens because once the furnace was turned on that's where they could be found cuddled up. It must have been quite a decision for them at night. Sleep in a nice comfy warm bed or on a hard floor that was toasty warm. I think they broke up their night between the two places.

Tim's Thanksgiving Soup

After we had our first Thanksgiving together, Tim started making this soup. I could not believe what he was doing with the leftovers. It took a lot of courage on my part to try his "masterpiece" but to my surprise it was excellent. Of course Tim knew that all along. It is a great way to use up all of the leftovers.

Ingredients you will need

1 Turkey Carcass
1 Cup Leftover Gravy (or 1 package)
2 Cups of Leftover Bread Stuffing
1 Onion - Diced
2 Carrots - Sliced
2 1/2 Quarts of Water
2 Celery Stalks - Sliced
4 Cloves of Garlic - Chopped
1 Teaspoon of Salt
1 Teaspoon of Pepper
1 Tablespoon of Powdered Chicken Base

How to Create Your Soup

Add all of the ingredients to a large soup pot at one time. Bring to a full boil and then skim the fat off of the top. Turn down the heat and simmer for about 1 1/2 hours. Remove the meat from the carcass and put back into the soup pot.

Of course this soup goes great with leftover biscuits and butter.

Thoughts, memories, recipes and notes:

_____

_____

_____

_____

_____

_____

_____

_____

_____

_____

_____

_____

_____

_____

_____

_____

_____

_____

_____

_____

_____

Precious Kittens

The kittens were so precious. Tim never had had a cat and Milo picked up on this immediately. He worked very hard to show Tim all he had been missing in his life by not having a furry feline. He and Millie would sit by the door and be the first thing Tim saw when he came home from a hard day at work. They would keep him company while he changed his clothes, join him for dinner and then relax with him in front of the television. Millie would curl up on the back of the couch and Milo would take his position cuddled in the crook of Tim's arm. As hard as Tim tried to deny it, he was well on his way to becoming a lover of cats.

Black-eyed Pea Soup

I first made this soup when I had a wonderful ham bone and no green split peas. The only peas on hand were black-eyed. I received funny looks but everyone really liked it. This soup is excellent served with a heaping plate of hot greens and sliced bread and butter.

Ingredients you will need

1 Tablespoon of Olive Oil
1 Tablespoon of Butter
1 Carrot - Sliced
2 Celery Stalks - Diced
1 Medium Onion - Diced
2 Large Cloves of Garlic - Minced
1 Ham Bone or Ham Hock
1 Tomato - Diced
1/4 Cup of Fresh Chopped Parsley
1 Tablespoon of Ham Stock (if needed)
1 Pound of Dry Black-eyed Peas
3 Quarts of Water
1 Tablespoon of Hot Sauce

How to Create Your Soup

Soak the peas for 4 hours and drain.

In olive oil and butter sauté the carrot, celery, onion and garlic cloves until tender. Usually about 10 minutes. Add the ham bone or ham hock, tomato, parsley, ham stock, black-eyed peas and water. Stir well and bring to a full boil. Boil 15 minutes then turn down the heat and simmer 1 1/2 hours. Check for seasonings. Add the hot sauce at this time to your taste. Take out the ham bone or ham hock and take the meat from it. Return the meat to the pot and warm through.

Thoughts, memories, recipes and notes:

_____

_____

_____

_____

_____

_____

_____

_____

_____

_____

_____

_____

_____

_____

_____

_____

_____

_____

_____

<u>Hot Fire</u>

When we moved into our new home it had a wonderful fireplace. Since Milo had never seen one before he made it his business to check out every aspect of it. He loved the warmth and would sit and stare into the flames for hours. It used to make me wonder what Milo was thinking about when lost in the glow of the fire. He did learn however that fire in the fireplace and fire from a candle were two very different things. Once while he was exploring, he walked over a burning candle. Well, needless to say cats are not fireproof. Milo's rear-end caught on fire and he started running around the house. I presume he was trying to outrun is rear-end. All you could see was a blur of black and white with smoke trailing behind. When we finally caught him and made sure that he was not injured, all he wanted was to be held. Thank goodness he wasn't physically injured. His pride, however, was another issue. From then on, candles held no purpose for Milo at all.

White Bean and Sausage Soup

This soup is so easy and tasty. The broth takes the flavor of the sausage. I've tried it with a ham bone and a ham hock and it's just not the same. Try either one, you may like them both.

Ingredients you will need

2 Cups of Dry Great Northern Beans
1 Tablespoon of Olive Oil
1 Tablespoon of Butter
2 Stalks of Celery - Diced
2 Carrots - Diced
1 Medium Onion - Diced
3 Cloves of Garlic - Minced
1 Pound of Smoked Polish Sausage (sliced)
1 Tablespoon of Chopped Fresh Parsley
1 - 16 Ounce Can Tomatoes - Drained and Cut Up
10 Cups of Cold Water

How to Create Your Soup

Soak the Great Northerns for 4 hours and drain.

In olive oil and butter sauté the carrots, celery, onion and garlic for 10 minutes or until tender. Add the sliced Polish sausage and cook until just slightly browned. Add the parsley, tomatoes, beans and water. Stir well and bring to a full boil. Boil 5 minutes and then turn down the heat and simmer 1 1/2 - 2 hours or until the beans are tender and the broth has started to thicken.

You don't need to add salt to this soup because of the sausage, but check for seasonings and if you wish to, go ahead and add salt and pepper.

Special Helper

I believe that, next to the fireplace, the kitchen was Milo's favorite place to be. I really think that cooking became so enjoyable for me because of Milo. If I were in the kitchen, so was Milo. He was interested in everything. It became a bond between us. We would talk and share all kinds of samples. I believe that Milo knew each recipe I made. Once, when Milo was very sick and could hardly walk, I was in the kitchen shredding zucchini to freeze for bread. I heard a little meow and there he was at my feet looking up. He didn't have the strength to jump, so I picked him up and placed him on the counter in his special spot. There he lay and watched. For that special moment everything was right again. To this day I have not used that zucchini I shredded that day. It remains in the freezer as a constant reminder of a special bond and a very special friend.

Dill Pickle Soup

I first had this soup in a Polish restaurant. I had never had it before and I found it quite interesting once I made the decision to try it. It is wonderful. All of the different flavors combined tastes truly great. Try It!!

Ingredients you will need

2 Tablespoons of Olive Oil
1 Large Clove of Garlic - Minced
1 Carrot - Finely Diced
1 Celery Stalk - Finely Diced
1 Medium Onion - Finely Diced
1 Whole Dill Pickle - Seeded and Diced
1 Potato - Diced
1/2 Teaspoon of Black Pepper
1/2 Teaspoon of Powdered Chicken Stock
1/4 Teaspoon of Salt
1/2 Teaspoon of Chopped Fresh Dill Weed
1 Teaspoon of Chopped Fresh Parsley
1/8 Teaspoon of Tarragon
1 Tablespoon of Pickle Juice
6 Cups of Water
1 Cup of Sour Cream
1 Tablespoon of Flour

How to Create Your Soup

In 2 tablespoons of olive oil sauté the garlic, carrot, celery, onion and dill pickle until soft, about 5-10 minutes. Add the potato, black pepper, chicken stock, salt, dill weed, parsley, tarragon, pickle juice and water. Bring to a full boil. Boil 15 minutes and then turn down and simmer about an hour or until the vegetables and diced pickles are tender.

To the 1 cup of sour cream add the flour and mix well. Add hot broth to the sour cream mixture and whisk well. Add slowly to the soup pot. Keep at a simmer until the soup has thickened. Do not boil.

This is great served with a nice loaf of dark rye bread.

Thoughts, memories, recipes and notes:

_____

_____

_____

_____

_____

_____

_____

_____

_____

_____

_____

_____

_____

_____

_____

_____

_____

_____

_____

_____

_____

Flowers

One thing I could never keep in the house were flowers of any kind. If there were a fresh plant, Milo insisted that there was a hidden treasure in the bottom of the pot and would proceed to dig to the bottom to find it. If there were fresh flowers, I would find flower petals in every room of the house. I guess Milo thought they looked better that way. If there were dried flowers, the straw dust would be all over the house. He would run through the house with flowers in his mouth as if he were carrying the Olympic torch. We're still finding flowers in the strangest places. After Milo left us we found a dried flower on the fireplace where he used to love to lie. We now have it in a small plastic container next to his picture, so he will always have it near.

Lima Bean Soup

Tim wanted this soup just out-of-the-blue one day. I had never made it, nor did I think I wanted to. As I started putting it together, I was amazed at how easy it was, and then how delicious. It really is a wonderfully rich and hearty combination.

Ingredients you will need

1 Tablespoon of Butter
1 Tablespoon of Olive Oil
2 Stalks of Celery - Diced
2 Carrots - Diced
3 Cloves of Garlic - Mashed
1 Medium Onion - Diced
1 Tablespoon of Chopped Fresh Parsley
1 Teaspoon of Salt
1 Teaspoon of White Pepper
1 Ham Bone or Ham Hock
1 Pound Bag of Dry Lima Beans
12 Cups of Water
3 Tablespoons of Sour Cream

How to Create Your Soup

Soak the lima beans for 4 hours and drain.

In butter and olive oil sauté the celery, carrots, garlic, onion and parsley. Add the salt, white pepper, ham bone or ham hock, lima beans and water. Bring to a full boil and boil 10 minutes. Turn down the heat and simmer 2 hours or until the beans are tender and the soup has started to thicken. To the 3 tablespoons of sour cream add some hot broth and mix well. Add back to the soup pot and whisk in until well blended. Keep at a simmer until nice and thick, but do not boil.

I love fresh dill weed, but I decided to keep it out of this soup. If you wish to add it, go right ahead, I'm sure it will be a nice addition.

Best Friends

Since we got the kittens, Millie and Milo were inseparable. They ate, played and slept together. Milo would place a paw on Millie to hold her down and give her a daily bath, she in turn would do the same for him. Millie could never jump as high as Milo and never tried (thank goodness), so Milo would go off exploring high places. But when it came down to serious sleep-time, they could always be found wrapped around each other somewhere in the house.

Old Fashioned Beef Dumpling Soup

This is such a flavorful soup. Use any cut of beef you choose. I just use chuck and it is great!

Ingredients you will need

1 Tablespoon of Olive Oil
1 Tablespoon of Butter
1 Pound of Chuck - cut into pieces
3 Meaty Soup Bones
1 Large Onion - Chopped
4 Celery Stalks - Chopped
4 Cloves of Garlic - Chopped
4 Carrots - Chopped
2 Bay Leaves
1 Teaspoon of Black Pepper
1 Teaspoon of Salt
3 Medium Potatoes - Diced
1/2 Pound of Dry Lima Beans
2 1/2 Quarts of Water

How to Create Your Soup

In olive oil and butter sauté the beef, onion, celery, garlic and carrots about 10 minutes. Add all of the other remaining ingredients and bring to a full boil. Boil 15 minutes then turn down the heat and simmer 1 1/2 to 2 hours.

The last hour check for seasonings and add some beef stock at this time if you feel it is needed.

Pull out your soup bones, pull off the meat and add back to the soup pot. (Give the soup bones to your kitty or your puppy.)

Keep at a simmer while you are preparing your dumplings. (The recipe will be later in the book.)

White Nose

Since the incident with the split peas, Milo usually left all dry beans alone so I never had to worry about that. He did, however, love the soup bones after they were taken out of the soup pot. It was a great treat for him that would keep him very busy for several hours.

By the time I was done making the dumplings, my little helper Milo would be covered in flour. His little black nose suddenly white. What a precious memory!

Cream of Tomato Soup

I tried may times to make a tomato soup and could never get the hang of it. I never was happy with the results. Well, I kept going and finally made a soup that even Tim was willing to try again. The recipe looks like a lot of work, but it is well worth it!

Ingredients you will need

2 Pounds of Pork Neck Bones
4 Cloves of Garlic
1 Medium Onion
4 Cups Peeled and Seeded Chopped Tomatoes
1/2 Cup of Finely Diced Celery
2 Tablespoons of Dry Red Wine (Optional)
1 Teaspoon of Salt
1/4 Teaspoon of Celery Salt
1 Cup of Sour Cream
1 Tablespoon of Chopped Fresh Parsley
2 Tablespoons of Olive Oil
2 Tablespoons of Butter
2 Quarts of Water
1- 6 Ounce Can of Tomato Paste
1/4 Teaspoon of White Pepper
2 Tablespoons of Flour
1 Tablespoon of Chopped Fresh Celery Leaves
1 Tablespoon of Fresh Chopped Dill

How to Create Your Soup

In a 350 degree oven place the neck bones, onion and garlic. Add 2 tablespoons of olive oil and bake for an hour. When the onion and garlic are cool, chop them up.

Peel and seed 4 cups of fresh tomatoes. Set aside.

In 2 tablespoons of butter sauté the celery, onion and garlic. Add the neck bones, 2 quarts of water and 2 tablespoons of dry red wine. Bring to a full boil, skim off the top and soft-boil 1/2 hour. Add the fresh tomatoes. Bring back to a full boil and smash down a little with your spoon. Add the celery leaves, parsley, dill and tomato paste. Simmer 1/2 hour. Add the salt, white pepper and celery salt.

To 1 cup of sour cream add 2 tablespoons of flour and mix well. Add hot broth to the sour cream and blend until smooth. Add slowly back to the soup and whisk well. Bring to a simmer.

Serve with fresh chopped dill sprinkled on top.

Thoughts, memories, recipes and notes:

_____

_____

_____

_____

_____

_____

_____

_____

_____

_____

_____

_____

_____

_____

_____

_____

_____

_____

_____

_____

_____

<u>Time to Get Up</u>

Milo believed that if he were up, everyone in the house had to be up also. He devised a tactic that worked 95% of the time. He would sit on the headboard and start shaking the mini blinds. I would yell at him to stop. He would jump down. This repeated itself many times over until you finally gave up and got up. Then content in the fact that he won and you were up, he would jump down and go about his daily business. He never wanted anything, he just didn't want you sleeping anymore.

Yellow Split Pea with Meatballs

I had such a taste for split pea soup and did not have green split peas. I did have yellow peas, though. So this soup came to be. It is so thick and creamy. You definitely do not need anything else to go with it.

Ingredients you will need for your soup

2 Tablespoons of Olive Oil
2 Tablespoons of Butter
2 Celery Stalks with Leaves - Sliced
2 Carrots - Sliced
1 Medium Onion - Minced
2 Cloves of Garlic - Minced
1 Ham Bone or Ham Hock
2 1/2 Quarts of Water
1 Bag of Yellow Split Peas
1/4 Teaspoon of White Pepper
1/4 Teaspoon of Red Pepper
2 Potatoes - Diced
3/4 Cup of Sour Cream

Ingredients you will need for the Meat Balls

1 Pound of Ground Pork
1 clove of Garlic - Minced
1 Small Onion - Minced
1/4 Teaspoon of Sage
1 Teaspoon of Chopped Fresh Parsley
1/4 Teaspoon of Salt
1/4 Teaspoon of Pepper
1 Egg
Dry Bread Crumbs

How to Create The Meatballs

Mix ground pork, minced garlic, minced onion, sage, parsley, salt, pepper and egg together well. Add enough bread crumbs to hold together. Make walnut-size meatballs. Place in the refrigerator until ready to use.

How to Create Your Soup

Sauté the celery, carrots, onion and garlic in olive oil and butter. Add the ham bone or ham hock, water, split peas, white pepper and red pepper. Bring to a full boil and then turn down and simmer 1 1/2 hours.

When the soup is nice and thick and the beans are tender, add the potatoes and the meatballs. Bring to a full boil and then reduce and simmer 1/2 hour. Stir often and watch carefully as it will stick to the bottom of the pot.

Take out the meatballs. (So be sure to count them when you make them.) Add 3/4 cup of sour cream and mix well with a whisk. Return the meatballs to the soup pot. Bring just to a soft boil and serve.

Since this soup is so hearty, you can serve just something simple like sliced tomatoes or sliced cucumbers as a side dish.

911

There is one thing Milo learned and took great pride in. He learned how to dial 911. Unfortunately it was 3 a.m. My telephone rang and the police were asking if there were a problem. After explaining that there was no problem, all was fine, I lay back down. Then the second call came in from the same dispatcher. Again she was told that I had not called 911. When I hung up and was about to lie back down I noticed Milo. He was by the telephone. He took his paw and tilted the received so he could hear the dial tone. I think he liked the noise it made. What he didn't know is that his back paw was on the preprogrammed 911 button. Before I could stop him he stepped on it a third time. This time the police dispatcher had lost all sense of humor. When I explained to her that it was not me calling 911 but my cat, she did not find that at all amusing. She informed me that 911 was an emergency number and not to be fooled with. She also told me to have a talk with my cat. Sure, I'll have a talk with Milo. She did not know Milo at all. Needless to say, the rest of the evening the telephone was unplugged.

Hamburger Soup

I first tasted this soup in a restaurant. Not knowing the recipe, I just guessed and tested until it was what I wanted. Actually this is such a versatile soup. Anything that grows in your garden can go into your soup pot. I have given you a basic recipe, but use your imagination and you will be surprised at how great a soup you can create. I love to use sour cream but I have had it without; it is super either way.

Ingredients you will need

5 Cloves of Garlic
1 Pound of Hamburger
1 Medium Onion - Diced
1 Tablespoon of Olive Oil
1 Tablespoon of Butter
2 Celery Stalks - Diced
2 Carrots - Diced
1/8 Teaspoon of Dill Weed
1/2 Teaspoon of Salt
1/2 Teaspoon of Pepper
1 Potato - Diced
1 Tomato - Diced
2 Cups of Chopped Fresh Spinach
2 1/2 Quarts of Water
1/2 Cup of Barley
1 Tablespoon of Dry Beef Stock
1/4 Cup of Sour Cream
2 Tablespoons of Chopped Fresh Parsley

How to Create Your Soup

In a 350 degree oven roast the garlic in a little olive oil until nicely brown. Cool and chop.

Brown the hamburger and onion in olive oil and butter. When almost browned add the celery, carrots, dill weed, salt, pepper and parsley. Sauté 5-10 minutes. Stir in the roasted chopped garlic. Add the potato, tomato and chopped fresh spinach. Stir well. Add 2 1/2 quarts of water. Bring to a full boil and then turn down and simmer 1 hour.

Add 1/2 cup of barley and check at this time for seasonings. Add the dry beef stock now if needed.

Soft boil an hour more or until the barley is tender and the soup has thickened.

Add some hot broth to the sour cream and stir well. Slowly add to the soup pot. Mix well and heat through. Try not to boil!

As I said earlier, you do not need to add the sour cream; I just found that it gives it an extra flavor that I enjoy.

USE YOUR IMAGINATION!!!

Thoughts, memories, recipes and notes:

_____

_____

_____

_____

_____

_____

_____

_____

_____

_____

_____

_____

_____

_____

_____

_____

_____

_____

_____

_____

_____

The Garden

When we moved from the attic apartment to a home in the suburbs, the garden was the first on our list of wishes. Milo could not believe all the wonderful and fun things that came out of it. I was never allowed to cook alone or unsupervised, so Milo would sit on the kitchen counter and inspect each ingredient that went into the pot.

Hamburger soup seemed to be one of his favorites because it took some time to prepare the vegetables. Actually, a lot of the time was spent retrieving the vegetables that seemed to jump off of the counter. Then they became Milo's newest toy. He would sit below while I peeled the potatoes and try swatting the peelings when they fell. He was usually quite good at catching, and then he and the peel would run off to play.

Grandma's Chicken Soup

My Grandmother Italia, would always make this soup. It seemed as if a pot of it were always cooking on her stove. It is so easy and simple, but so very good. I love it. Once I got sick and she brought the entire pot over to me. There are so many ways to make chicken soup, but to me no matter how fancy you get, this is still my favorite. I think it's the little noodles she puts in it.

Ingredients you will need

1 Chicken
2 Celery Stalks - Sliced Long
2 Carrots - Sliced Long
1 Onion - Diced
1 Tomato - Diced
2 16-Ounce Cans of Chicken Broth
2 Quarts of Water
Angel Hair Pasta

Parmesan Cheese - Grated
Chopped Fresh Parsley

How to Create Your Soup

Add the chicken, celery, carrots, onion, tomato, chicken broth and water to your pot. Bring to a full boil. Turn down and simmer 1 1/2 hours. Take the chicken out and take the meat from the bones and put the meat back into the soup.

In a separate pot cook the angel hair pasta. Add that to the soup when done.

Serve with grated parmesan cheese and parsley sprinkled on the top.

I must confess that I always add ketchup to my chicken soup (to anyone's chicken soup). I think my sisters and brother do also.

This is one of the easiest soups to make. It's fast and delicious.

Thoughts, memories, recipes and notes:

_____

_____

_____

_____

_____

_____

_____

_____

_____

_____

_____

_____

_____

_____

_____

_____

_____

_____

_____

_____

_____

<u>Hugs for Sale</u>

Milo learned very early how to give hugs. He would get up on his hind legs, put a paw on each side of my neck and hug. He also learned very early on that this would get him out of almost any trouble he happened to be in at the time. What could be better in the middle of winter than a nice hot pot of Grandma's Chicken Soup and a warm hug from a very precious friend!

Tim's Chicken Soup and Dinner

Tim insists that this is the ONLY way to make chicken soup. He uses a stewing chicken and then makes a wonderful dinner along with it.

Ingredients you will need

1 Stewing Chicken
4 Celery Stalks - Sliced
4 Cloves of Garlic - Chopped
1 Bay Leaf
4 Carrots - Sliced
1 Onion - Diced
1/2 Cup of Fresh Chopped Parsley
2 Quarts of Water
1 Tablespoon of Dry Chicken Stock
2 Onions - Sliced
2 Tablespoons of Butter
1 Package of Chicken Gravy

How to Create Your Soup

Place the stewing chicken, celery, garlic, bay leaf, carrots, 1 chopped onion, parsley and water in a soup pot. Bring to a full boil. Then turn down and simmer about 2 hours or until the stewing chicken is tender. Check at this time. If the dry chicken stock is needed, add now. Take out the chicken and set aside.

Then

Remove the chicken to a roaster. Sauté 2 sliced onions in butter and pour over the chicken. Mix one package of chicken gravy with 1 1/2 cups of water and mix well. Pour the gravy mixture over the onions and chicken. Cover and bake in a 350 degree oven about 30 minutes or until heated through. You now have chicken soup and a nice chicken dinner.

Make flour dumplings for your soup. Tim insists that it's not finished until the little dumplings are in it.

<u>Merry Christmas</u>

Christmas was just the cats pajamas to Milo. One year we went out and bought our first artificial tree. We decided against a real one because we did not want any of the animals getting hurt by eating the pine needles. We had it decorated so nicely. I remember one day sitting at the kitchen table and noticing that the tree was moving. I could not see anything though. I went over to the tree and there was Milo in the center of it lying on one of the branches. I tried to coax him out but he was not at all interested. Well, that branch came tumbling down along with one very startled kitty. To this day the tree is still broken. But every time I see it, it only brings a smile to my face. I would not fix that tree for anything.

Mary's French Onion Soup

This is my sister Mary's recipe for French Onion Soup. Sure you could cook over a stove all day making your beef stock, but why would you want to when you can make a wonderful soup this easily? I've made it several times, but I must confess it seems to taste better when Mary makes it and serves it to me.

Ingredients you will need

6 - 8 Onions - Sliced Thin
1/2 to 1 Stick of Margarine - Melted
3 Tablespoons of Flour
3 Cans of Beef Consommé
3 Soup Cans of Water
1 Can Dry White Wine (Chablis is fine)
Sliced French Bread
Slices of Swiss Cheese
Salt and Pepper to Taste

How to Create Your Soup

Cook the onions in melted margarine until limp.
Sprinkle with flour and stir until golden brown but not
dark brown. Add consommé, water and wine. Bring to
a boil, stirring uncovered about 20 minutes. Add salt
and pepper. Place bread in oven-proof individual
bowls. Pour hot soup over it. Add cheese slice to
cover (I like a lot of cheese). Broil until the cheese is
melted and golden.

Of course this soup goes great with a nice chilled glass
of white wine.

<u>Sniper Attacks</u>

Milo had what we called sniper attacks. Tim was usually the victim. Milo would scope him out, then in one leap and without advance warning, he would land on his shoulders and wrap himself around his neck. It really did not matter to him if Tim were comfortable or not. To Milo, it felt great!

Sauerkraut Soup

This soup is so good. It's not a heavy soup, but a hearty soup. It tastes even better the next day.

Ingredients you will need

1 Pound of Pork Neck Bones
1 Onion
1 Tablespoon of Olive Oil
2 Celery Stalks - Finely Chopped
2 Carrots - Finely Chopped
2 Cloves of Garlic - Finely Chopped
1/2 Head of Cabbage - Finely Sliced
1 Teaspoon of Salt
1 Teaspoon of Pepper
1 Bay Leaf
10 Peppercorns
2 Tablespoons of Maggi
2 1/2 Quarts of Water
1 Tablespoon of Chopped Fresh Dill
1 Tablespoon of Chopped Fresh Parsley
1 Cup of Sauerkraut (undrained)
2 Potatoes - Diced
1 Tomato - Seeded, Peeled and Chopped
1 10-Ounce Can of Chicken Broth

Fresh Dill - Chopped (Optional)

How to Create Your Soup

In a 350 degree oven, bake the neck bones and onion in 1 tablespoon of olive oil about 30 minutes. When the onion is cool, chop it up.

Sauté in a separate pot, 2 tablespoons of olive oil, celery, carrots, garlic, 1/2 head of cabbage, 1 teaspoon of salt and 1 teaspoon of pepper about 1/2 hour or until tender.

In your soup pot add the neck bones, chopped onion, 1 bay leaf, peppercorns, 2 tablespoons of Maggi and 2 1/2 quarts of water. Bring to a full boil for 15 minutes.

Add the cabbage mixture, 1 tablespoon of dill and 1 tablespoon of parsley. Cover and boil 1/2 hour.

Add 1 cup of sauerkraut, 2 potatoes, 1 tomato and 1 can of chicken broth.

Bring to a full boil then turn down and simmer 1/2 hour to 45 minutes. Salt and pepper to taste at this time.

Serve with chopped fresh dill sprinkled on the top.

Special Comfort

Milo made it his business to know everything that was going on. If you were happy, Milo was happy. If you were sad or not feeling well, this truly upset Milo. I remember once when I had a bad case of the blues. Milo never left my side. I was lying on the couch and he walked up my chest and just stared at me. He would lie there as long as he felt I needed him, his patience never giving up.

Beef Barley Soup

I don't make this soup very often because Tim is not a big fan of barley. But I love it. Because of the barley this soup cooks itself. I like to finely chop the vegetables as it seems to make a creamier and thicker soup. Serve with piping hot fresh bread and butter for a meal in itself.

Ingredients you will need

1 Tablespoon of Olive Oil
1 Tablespoon of Butter
1/2 Pound of Beef - Cubed - (Pot Roast is Fine)
1 Large Onion - Finely Diced
1 Carrot - Finely Diced
1 Celery Stalk - Finely Diced
1/2 Cup of Barley
2 Garlic Cloves - Roasted and Chopped
1/2 Teaspoon of Salt
1/2 Teaspoon of Pepper
1 Tablespoon of Chopped Fresh Parsley
1 Potato - Diced
2 1/2 Quarts of Water
2 16-Ounce Cans of Beef Broth
1 Small Jar of Sliced Mushrooms

How to Create Your Soup

Roast the garlic in a little olive oil in a 350 degree oven for 20 minutes. Take out and cool.

In olive oil and butter sauté the beef, onion, carrot, celery and barley until nice and golden brown. This usually takes about 10 - 15 minutes. Add the roasted garlic, salt, pepper, fresh parsley and potato. Mix well. Add the water, 1 can of beef broth and the mushrooms.

Bring to a full boil. Turn down and simmer 1 1/2 - 2 hours or until the barley is tender and the soup has started to thicken.

Add the other can of beef broth at this time if the soup is too thick.

Don't forget your hot fresh bread and butter!

Stress Test

One day Tim worked for hours putting shelves up on a wall, on which to arrange some of our treasures. When he asked if I thought they were strong enough, Milo decided to help us with that decision. With one leap onto a shelf, Milo-style, all came tumbling down. So, out went the shelves and in came bookcases. Those passed the Milo stress test!

Lentil Soup

I am not a big fan of lentils, but when my sister Kimberly keeps asking for this soup, I know it must be a good pot of soup. Again, in this soup, the finer you dice the vegetables the creamier your soup will be. But if you like chunky vegetables, that's OK too.

Ingredients you will need

1 Tablespoon of Olive Oil
1 Tablespoon of Butter
2 Carrots - Finely Diced
2 Celery Stalks - Finely Diced
1 Clove of Garlic - Finely Diced
1 Medium Onion - Finely Diced
1 Ham Bone or Ham Hock
1 Pound Bag of Dried Lentils
1 Potato - Finely Diced
1 Tablespoon of Chopped Fresh Parsley
1/2 Teaspoon of Pepper
2 Quarts of Water
1 Tomato - Diced
Sour Cream

74-

How to Create Your Soup

In olive oil and butter sauté the carrots, celery, garlic and onions until limp. Add all of the other ingredients except tomato and sour cream. Bring to a full boil. Turn down and simmer 1 hour. Add the chopped tomato and simmer another 30 minutes until thick and rich.

Serve with a dollop of sour cream in the center.

<u>Welcome Home</u>

Milo was a definite handful, but I found myself missing him when I was not at home. I knew that when I opened the door he would be there. It did not matter to him what I looked like or what kind of mood I was in. He could change the darkest skies in a second. And I truly believe that he knew that. Sometimes I think he knew he did not have long on this earth and gave it his all to show how important a happy life is.

Cream of Vegetable Soup

This soup is so easy. If you have all the vegetables in your garden, use them. If not, use frozen. Either way, you end up with a nice, thick, warming soup. In this soup I like to leave the vegetables chopped or chunky. The texture seems to be better and it looks so much prettier.

Ingredients you will need

2 Tablespoons of Olive Oil
2 Tablespoons of Butter
1 Medium Onion - Chopped
2 Large Cloves of Garlic - Chopped
3 Green Onions - Sliced Thin
1 Carrot - Diced
1 Celery Stalk with Leaves - Diced
2 Jalapeno Peppers - Minced
1 Tablespoon of Fresh Chopped Dill
1 Tablespoon of Fresh Chopped Parsley
1 Cup of Frozen Corn
1 Cup of Frozen Lima Beans
1 Cup of Frozen Green Beans
1 Cup of Frozen Cauliflower
1 1/2 Quarts of Water
2 - 16 Ounce Cans of Vegetable Broth
1 Large Potato - Diced
1 Cup of Frozen Peas
1 Tomato - Diced
1 Cup of Sour Cream
1 Tablespoon of Flour

How to Create Your Soup

In olive oil and butter sauté the onion, garlic, green onions, carrot, celery and jalapeno peppers. Sauté about 7 - 10 minutes. Add the fresh dill and parsley and mix well. To this add the corn, lima beans, green beans, cauliflower, water and 2 cans of vegetable broth. Bring to a full boil. Boil 30 minutes. Add your potato and turn down and simmer 1/2 hour.

Add peas and tomato and bring back to a boil. Then turn down and simmer while you mix the sour cream mixture.

In a bowl add 1 tablespoon of flour and 1 cup of sour cream. Mix well. Add some hot broth to the mixture and whisk well. Add back to the soup pot and simmer until nice and thick.

Serve with freshly ground pepper on top.

Thoughts, memories, recipes and notes:

_____

_____

_____

_____

_____

_____

_____

_____

_____

_____

_____

_____

_____

_____

_____

_____

_____

_____

_____

_____

_____

New Name

Milo got to be quite the celebrity when he became ill. He spent so much time in the vet's office that I'm sure it began to feel like a second home to him. One of the vets called him Mr. MiMi. That unfortunately seemed to stick with him. Tim and I even started calling him Mr. Mi. I'm not quite sure Milo liked that name. I think he preferred to be called Mr. Milo.

Cream of Potato Soup

This soup just came about because I had things in the refrigerator that needed to be put to use. So you see, you can make a soup out of anything you have left over. Try it, use your imagination. Sure, some things won't always work out but you'd be surprised when they do.

Ingredients you will need

5 Bacon Strips
1 Tablespoon of Olive Oil
1 Tablespoon of Butter
3 Celery Stalks with Leaves - Chopped
1 Medium Onion - Chopped
4 Cloves of Garlic - Chopped
2 Cups of finely Sliced Cabbage
4 Cups of Diced Potato
2 Teaspoons of Horseradish
2 Quarts of Water
1/4 Teaspoon of Dill Weed
1/2 Teaspoon of Mrs. Dash Lemon Pepper
1/8 Teaspoon (or more) of Chili Powder
1 Tablespoon of Maggi
1 Tablespoon of Flour
1 Cup of Sour Cream

Vinegar (Optional)
Dill (Optional)

How to Create Your Soup

Fry the bacon in your soup pot. Take out and set aside. Add the olive oil and butter, celery, onion, garlic and cabbage. Sauté about 15 minutes or until the cabbage starts to wilt. Add all of the other ingredients except the sour cream and flour. Bring to a full boil and boil 15 minutes. Turn down and simmer 1 hour.

Add the flour to the sour cream and mix well. Add some hot broth to the sour cream and then add back to the soup pot. Simmer until nice and thick and rich.

I also added at the very end 2 tablespoons of vinegar. That, of course, is optional. I just like the tart taste it gives the soup.

Serve with a little dill sprinkled on the top.

Thoughts, memories, recipes and notes:

Bird at Large

In the winter Milo loved the fireplace and it was not odd to find him there in front of it. But one day in the summer, I found him sitting and staring into the fireplace for the longest time. I kept going over to see what was wrong. He would not budge. So I decided to show him that there was nothing in there that would interest him at all. When I opened the flue, out came a black bird! Well, one broken lamp later and with everything knocked off of the counters, we finally caught the bird. We had just painted the kitchen and there were black marks on the ceiling and the walls. Since then whenever I saw Milo totally engrossed in something, I learned to proceed with caution.

Fresh Chunky Tomato Soup

This is a different twist to tomato soup. It comes out very thick and rich. It can get a little tart, depending on your tomatoes, so adjust the amount of sugar to your liking.

Ingredients you will need

2 Pounds of Pork Neck Bones
4 Cloves of Garlic
1 Medium Onion
2 Tablespoons of Olive Oil
1 Celery Stalk - Diced
1 Cup of Sauerkraut - Unrinsed and Undrained
4 Cups of Peeled and Seeded Tomatoes
2 Medium Potatoes - Diced
1 6 - Ounce Can of Tomato Paste
1 Tablespoon of Chopped Fresh Dill
2 Quarts of Water
1 Tablespoon of Salt
1/2 Tablespoon of Pepper
1 Teaspoon of Maggi
1 Teaspoon to 1 Tablespoon of Sugar

How to Create Your Soup

Place the neck bones, onion and garlic in a small roasting pan. Pour olive oil over and bake in a 350 degree oven until nice and brown. Take out and cool. Then chop up the onion and mash the garlic.

In your soup pot place the neck bones, onion, garlic, celery and 2 quarts of water. Bring to a full boil and then turn down and simmer 1 hour.

Add the 4 cups of tomatoes, 1 cup of sauerkraut, 2 small diced potatoes, 1 can of tomato paste, 1 tablespoon of dill, 1 tablespoon of salt and 1/2 Tablespoon of pepper. Simmer another hour. Taste now for the amount of sugar you will need and add until correct. Add the teaspoon of Maggi and simmer another 15 minutes.

Of course a nice bowl of Tomato Soup goes great with a nice grilled cheese sandwich!

Thoughts, memories, recipes and notes:

_____

_____

_____

_____

_____

_____

_____

_____

_____

_____

_____

_____

_____

_____

_____

_____

_____

_____

_____

<u>Shampoo Time</u>

Milo had a really bizarre habit. Thank goodness Tim was the only one who interested him when he got the urge. He would wait until Tim was lying down and then he would put a paw on each side of Tim's head and proceed to clean his hair. All of it! He would not stop until each hair had been attended to. Then he would just get up and walk away. Tim would end up with soaking wet hair. I never mentioned this to Tim, but maybe Milo was trying to tell him something??????????????????

What's Cooking in Salads

Marinated Onions
Mom's Potato Salad
Orange Spinach Salad
Leftover Meat Salad
Garlic Roasted Peppers
Fresh Mushrooms in Sour Cream
Pickled Beets
Cold Beets in Sour Cream and Dill
Endive Salad
Marinated Tomato Salad
Marinated Mushroom Salad
Tri-Colored Pepper Salad
Auntie Mary's Cole Slaw
Paper Thin Cucumbers
Kidney Bean Salad

Marinated Onion Salad

You really have to love onions to enjoy this salad. I must admit I was a little skeptical at first, but I had all these onions and nothing to do with them.

Ingredients you will need

2 Large Onions - Sliced Very Thin
3 Green Onions - Sliced Very Thin
1/4 Cup of Chopped Fresh Parsley
Olive Oil to Taste
Vinegar to Taste
1/2 Teaspoon of Sugar
1/4 Teaspoon of Dry Mustard
1/2 Teaspoon of Salt
1/2 Teaspoon of White Pepper

How to Prepare Your Salad

Slice the onions and green onions and set aside in a large mixing bowl.

Combine the olive oil and vinegar. Add the sugar, dry mustard, salt and white pepper. Mix well.

Toss the onions with the parsley. Add the dressing and toss well. Leave at room temperature 1 - 2 hours. (or if you prefer, you can chill the same amount of time.)

Mom's Potato Salad

My mom, Yvonne, has been making this potato salad for as long as I can remember. Everywhere she takes it, someone asks for the recipe. It is truly excellent!

Ingredients you will need

5 Pounds of Medium Size Red Potatoes
8 Hard-Boiled Eggs
1 Medium Onion - Chopped
1/2 Cup of Celery - Finely Chopped
1/2 Pint of Sour Cream
8 - Ounce Jar of Mayonnaise
1/2 Can of Condensed Milk
Salt and Pepper to Taste

How to Prepare Your Salad

Boil the potatoes until tender. Drain and peel. Cut up into chunks. Add 6 hard-boiled eggs, chopped onion, celery, salt and pepper. Mix well.

In separate bowl mix the sour cream, mayonnaise and condensed milk and add to the potatoes. Slice the remaining 2 eggs for garnish. You can change the amount of the ingredients to your taste.

Sprinkle a little parsley and paprika on the top for garnish.

Orange Spinach Salad

This is my version of spinach salad minus the eggs. It's a little different, but tastes so fresh.

Ingredients you will need

1 Bag of Fresh Spinach - Washed and Cut Up
4 - 5 Slices of Bacon
1 Red Onion - Cut into Paper Thin Slices
1 Small Can of Mandarin Oranges
1 Tablespoon of Lemon Juice
Diced Egg White - Optional

How to Prepare Your Salad

Wash and cut the spinach into bite-size pieces. Fry the bacon until just crisp. Take out the bacon strips and set aside to cool. To the hot bacon grease add the juice of the mandarin oranges and the lemon juice. Boil and reduce to 1/3. Crumble the bacon and add to the juice mixture.

Toss the mandarin oranges, red onion and spinach. Add the hot, cooked sauce and toss well. Sprinkle with the chopped egg white if you choose.

Thoughts, memories, recipes and notes:

_____

_____

_____

_____

_____

_____

_____

_____

_____

_____

_____

_____

_____

_____

_____

_____

_____

_____

_____

_____

_____

_____

Time to Wallpaper

Not only was the kitchen where Milo helped out. He once decided to help me out when I was wallpapering the bedroom. Every time I stepped down from the ladder I had to step over him because he would not move from his supervising position. When the telephone rang and I left to answer it, you can imagine what I found when I returned. There was my nicely cut and wet wallpaper wrapped around a very surprised Milo. It got stuck to him and he couldn't even run to escape it. After finally convincing him I could help, he lay there and waited to be unglued. After that he supervised from a more distant position.

Leftover Meat Salad

It's hard to write down ingredients for this salad because it really is what the title says. Leftovers. It's made with anything you have leftover but not enough for another meal. The amounts of the vegetables and the amounts of dressing depends upon the amount of leftovers you are working with. You'll have fun with this salad. It will change each time you make it.

Ingredients you will need

Any Leftover Meat - Pork, Chicken, Beef
Chopped Seeded Tomato
Onion (Any Kind You Have)
Green, Red or Yellow Pepper
Celery - Diced Fine
Carrot - Diced Fine
Any Cheese you may have
Fresh Chopped Parsley
Garlic Cloves - Diced Fine
Fresh Green Beans or Corn
ANYTHING

Ingredients for your dressing

Balsamic Vinegar
Olive Oil
Dijon Mustard
Oregano - Just a Touch
Garlic - Mashed with Salt
Drops of Hot Sauce
Touch of Paprika

Whisk the amount of vinegar you like into about 1/3 cup of olive oil. Add the remaining ingredients to your taste and whisk well. Set aside.

How to Prepare Your Salad

Dice the meat into bite-size pieces and place in a glass bowl. Add the rest of the ingredients and mix all together well.

Add the salad dressing slowly. Don't drown the salad. Just lightly coat and mix well. Place in the refrigerator and chill about an hour. Mix well again before serving.

I like to serve a scoop of this salad over a bed of lettuce leaves. It looks so pretty.

Serve with a nice loaf of Italian Bread and butter.

Garlic Roasted Peppers

These peppers are wonderful on a cold winter's night. Eating them at room temperature enhances the flavor. I love them on top of a slice of Italian Bread with a little parsley and parmesan cheese sprinkled on the top.

Ingredients you will need

1 Green, Yellow and Red Pepper
5 Cloves of Unpeeled Garlic
Olive Oil
Fresh Parsley
Parmesan Cheese

How to Prepare Your Peppers

Pour 1/4 - 1/2 cup of olive oil over the peppers and garlic. Roast them whole in a 375 degree oven until the skins on the peppers are almost black. Take out and place in a small brown paper bag. Let sit in the bag for 15 minutes.

Take the peppers out and peel the skins from them. Peel the garlic. Seed and slice the peppers into large strips. Mash the roasted garlic.

Add 1/4 cup of olive oil to the roasted garlic. Pour over the peppers and add chopped fresh parsley. Marinate at room temperature 2 hours.

Sprinkle with a little fresh parsley and parmesan cheese.

Fresh Mushrooms in Sour Cream

This is a great addition to pork chops or beef. The smell of fresh mushrooms and onions cooking is irresistible.

Ingredients you will need

1 Tablespoon of Olive Oil
1 Tablespoon of Butter
1 Pound of Fresh Mushrooms - Sliced
1/2 Cup of Sour Cream
1 Medium Onion - Sliced
1 Teaspoon (or more) of Worcestershire Sauce
1/8 Teaspoon of Sugar

How to Prepare Your Mushrooms

Melt olive oil and butter in a large frying pan. Add the sliced mushrooms and onions and gently sauté until tender. Usually about 15 - 20 minutes. Stir in the Worcestershire sauce and sugar. Mix well. Add the sour cream and continue stirring until nice and creamy. Bring just to a boil. Cook about 10 minutes on low heat.

Serve either on top of your meat, or as a nice side dish to compliment your meal.

<u>Beware of Leaves</u>

Milo was never let outside. But when we were out in the garden or just sitting at the picnic table, he would get on his hind legs and start pounding on the door. He would not stop until he got our attention. One time he did this so long we decided to bring him outside and see what he would do. So Tim went and picked him up and set him on the picnic table. He looked around, smelled the scents and looked at the sun. Then when the first leaf blew across the grass, he took off and headed straight for the door. I guess things looked better to him on the inside looking out.

Pickled Beets

I just love pickled beets. They last so long in the refrigerator. Actually they get better the longer they sit. Which isn't too long in my house. For the best taste, slice the beets and onions as thin as you can get them.

Ingredients you will need

5 Medium Beets - Sliced Very Thin
1 Small Onion - Sliced Very Thin
1/2 Cup of White Vinegar
1/3 Cup of Sugar
1 Teaspoon of Salt
1/8 Teaspoon of Pepper

How to Prepare Your Beets

Slice the beets and onions very thin. In a large sauce pan add the vinegar, sugar, salt and pepper. Bring to a full boil. Add the beets and the onions. Bring back to a full boil and boil 10 minutes. Turn off the heat and let the mixture cool. Keep in a sealed container in the refrigerator until ready to use.

Cold Beets in Sour Cream Dill Sauce

There is nothing better than fresh picked beets and fresh picked dill. But if you have a taste for this in the winter, chill a can of beets and use them in place of fresh.

Ingredients you will need

6 Fresh Beets (or 1 Can of Beets)
1/2 Cup of Sour Cream
1 Tablespoon of Chopped Fresh-Picked Dill
Just a Touch of Salt and Pepper

How to Prepare Your Salad

Add beets to a pot and cover with water. Bring to a boil and boil until tender. The amount of time depends on the size of the beets you are using. Just prick them with a knife; if the knife goes in easily they are done. Drain and cool to the touch. Pull the peelings from the beets and cube.

Mix the sour cream, dill, salt and pepper. Pour over the beets and gently mix together. Let chill about 1/2 hour. I guarantee there won't be any leftovers.

If you use canned beets, drain and chill.

Prepare the same way as fresh.

Endive Salad

I don't measure anything that goes into this salad. It depends on how many you are making it for and your own personal tastes. If you like a lot of tomatoes, add another. If you like eggs, add another. It all depends on you. The same goes for the dressing. Start with mayonnaise and go from there.

Ingredients you will need

Endive
Tomato
Cooked Egg White (or Entire Egg)
Freshly Grated Parmesan Cheese
Fresh Chopped Dill
Fresh Milled Pepper

Ingredients for your dressing

Mayonnaise
Wine Vinegar
Sugar

How to Prepare Your Salad

Take the endive and roll it up very tight. Then
julienne into fine strips. Add finely seeded and diced
tomato, one finely diced cooked egg white, or it you
prefer use the entire egg. Toss all with the grated
Parmesan cheese, fresh dill and fresh milled pepper.
Set aside.

Put the mayonnaise into a bowl. Add vinegar a little
at a time until it is to your liking. Then with a whisk
add your sugar. Again start out with a little and keep
tasting until you like the taste. Whisk well to
incorporate the sugar.

Add the dressing to the salad just before serving time.

Thoughts, memories, recipes and notes:

Hello Trooper

When we got our new puppy Trooper, a yellow
Labrador retriever, the house went into an uproar.
Trooper did not bother our 18-year-old cat Kelly, at
all. I guess he figured that at her age she had seen it
all. Millie and Milo were a different story. They had
never known a dog so this was quite an experience.
They would approach him all puffed up, as if to tell
him it was their house not his. Trooper was so mild
tempered that it did not phase him. When Milo got
brave enough, he would wait for Trooper to fall asleep,
then grab an ear and try to take off with it. Trooper
kept his sense of humor for a while, but eventually it
was time to tell the kitties that he was not only bigger,
but stronger than the both of them. Since that day,
home is a nice peaceful place to be.

Marinated Tomato Salad

This recipe has been in our family for years. It is also my favorite on a summer day. It is so refreshing on a hot afternoon with tomatoes just picked from the garden. I have tried making it with store-bought tomatoes, but it isn't the same. The salad can be chilled, but leaving it a room temperature really brings out the flavor of the fresh tomatoes.

Ingredients you will need

4 Large Fresh Tomatoes - Sliced 1/8" Thick
1 Medium Onion - Sliced Thin
1/2 Cup of Fresh Chopped Parsley
Your Favorite Brand of Italian Dressing

How to Prepare Your Salad

Slice the tomatoes and toss with the sliced onions and parsley. Mix well to coat the tomatoes with the parsley. Add as much of the bottled dressing as you like and mix gently until all is covered. Let sit on the kitchen counter for a couple of hours tossing every so often. This is a great side salad for a barbecue.

Marinated Mushroom Salad

This mushroom salad is so good when nicely chilled. Use canned or bottled mushrooms. They taste better in this recipe than fresh. It is a little spicy though, so beware.

Ingredients you will need

4 - 4 Ounce Jars of Button Mushrooms
3 Cloves of Garlic - Minced
Olive Oil
Red Wine Vinegar
1/4 Teaspoon of White Pepper
1/4 Teaspoon of Dry Mustard
1 Pinch of Sugar

How to Prepare Your Mushrooms

Add the mushrooms and the minced garlic in a glass bowl. In a separate bowl add the olive oil and vinegar to taste and whisk well together. Add the dry mustard and white pepper. Whisk well. (I also add a few drops of hot sauce.) Add a pinch of sugar and toss well.

Chill several hours and enjoy.

Great to take on a picnic!

Tri-Colored Pepper Salad

I think this salad is so pretty when finished. It is similar to the roasted peppers except you don't roast them. It is such a refreshing and crisp addition to either a nice bowl of soup or a warm winter meal. It seems to bring summer into a winter kitchen.

Ingredients you will need

1 Green, 1 Red and 1 Yellow Pepper
2 Cloves of Garlic - Minced
1/8 Cup of Olive Oil
1/4 Cup of Red Wine Vinegar
Fresh Parsley
Freshly Grated Parmesan Cheese

How to Prepare Your Salad

Julienne the peppers. Toss together with the minced garlic.

In a glass bowl, add the red wine vinegar. Slowly add the olive oil until it is the blend you enjoy. Stir in the fresh parsley and mix well. Toss the peppers with the dressing and chill 2 hours.

Top with fresh grated Parmesan cheese. It is so pretty!

Thoughts, memories, recipes and notes:

Auntie Mary's Cole Slaw

This is my Aunt Mary's favorite recipe for cole slaw. I asked her for it one time and I will give it to you exactly as she wrote it down for me.

Ingredients you will need

1 Large Cabbage - Shredded Fine
1 Large Onion - Sliced Thin
1/2 Cup of Sugar

In a large bowl, mix the above ingredients well.

In a sauce pan add

3/4 Cup of Cooking Oil
1/2 Cup of White Vinegar
1/2 Cup of Sugar
1 Teaspoon of Dry Mustard
1 Teaspoon of Celery Seed
1 Teaspoon of Salt

How to Prepare Your Cole Slaw

Boil the oil, vinegar, sugar, dry mustard, celery seed
and salt one minute. Pour over cabbage. DO NOT
MIX! Cover and refrigerate 4 hours or overnight. Can
be put into containers after the 4 hours and frozen. If
packaged properly the cole slaw can be frozen for 4-6
months. For color you can add 1/2 red pepper diced
very thin.

I did divide the cole slaw into 2 containers and put
them in the freezer. I didn't get to them for several
months, but the salad tasted as fresh as the day it was
made.

I did add the red pepper, chopped, and a little salt and
pepper before serving. It looked so nice when blended.

Paper Thin Cucumbers

I first had this when I visited one of my aunts. I was hungry and she gave me a Polish sausage sandwich, and on the side she served these cucumbers. It now has become a habit each time I have a Polish sausage sandwich. Try it, you'll love it too!!

Ingredients you will need

One Large Fresh-Picked Cucumber
White Vinegar
Olive Oil
Sugar

How to Prepare Your Cucumbers

Use a hand-held vegetable slicer-grater and run the cucumber over it into nice paper thin slices.

In separate bowl put the white vinegar and just a touch of olive oil. The vinegar depends on how large of a cucumber you sliced. Add about 1/2 teaspoon of sugar and mix until well blended.

Pour over the cucumbers and you can either chill them or, if you can't wait, eat them immediately.

Kidney Bean Salad

Tim loves kidney bean salad. Since I can't eat it because of the eggs involved, I really don't make it as often as I should. I think it is best made the day before you are going to serve it.

Ingredients you will need

1 Can of Red Kidney Beans (Rinsed)
2 Hard-Boiled Eggs - Diced
1 Stalk of Celery - Diced
1 Medium Onion - Diced
1/2 Teaspoon of Celery Seed
Salt and Pepper to Taste
1/2 Cup of Mayonnaise
1/2 Cup of Sour Cream

How to Prepare Your Kidney Beans

Place the drained can of kidney beans into a large bowl. Add 2 diced hard-boiled eggs, celery, onion, celery seed, salt and pepper. Stir together well.

In separate bowl add the mayonnaise and sour cream. Mix well. Add to the kidney bean mixture and blend well.

Chill several hours or overnight.

A Few Little Extras

Flour Dumplings
Bacon Buns
Bacon Corn Bread
Garlic Bagel Chips
HOT Greens

Flour Dumplings

These dumplings are a must for Tim. He has to have them in the Beef Soup and in his Chicken Soup. I love noodles, he loves dumplings. Well, I guess I could always split the soup in half.

Ingredients you will need

Flour
Egg
Chopped Fresh Parsley (Optional)
Salt
Pepper

How to Prepare Your Dumplings

It's hard to give this recipe. The amount of ingredients are not always the same. It depends on how many dumplings you want to make.

Basically, start out with one beaten egg. Add flour and keep mixing until you get the consistency of a sticky dough. Usually, if it runs off the spoon, you should keep adding flour. Add the parsley and the salt and pepper and mix well.

Bring your soup to a boil. Drop the dumpling batter by 1/8 teaspoons into the soup. Cover and boil about 15 minutes.

Bacon Buns

I love Lithuanian bacon buns but I don't like all the time and work it takes to make them. I wanted to devise a way to make them more easily. These are great served any time and with any soup you have cooking.

Ingredients you will need

1 Package Frozen Bread Rolls
1 Pound of Bacon
1 Large Onion
1/2 Pound of Ham

How to Prepare Your Bacon Buns

Thaw the rolls until workable.

Chop the bacon very fine and add to a large fry pan. Add the chopped onion and fry until both are just limp but cooked enough. Add the chopped ham and just heat through.

Take each roll and roll to about 1/8" thick. Use about 2 tablespoons of the bacon mixture and place on the edge of the roll. Fold over the edges and then fold in the sides. Roll until completely sealed. Place seam-side down on a cookie sheet. Let rise until double.

Place in a 350 degree oven for about 30 minutes or until the tops are nicely browned.

Take out and cool.

If you can wait that long!!

Bacon Corn Bread

This goes so well with any hearty meal. The aroma of the bacon cooking just makes your mouth water.

Ingredients you will need

3 Slices of Bacon
1/4 Cup of Oil
1 Cup of Cornmeal
1 Cup of Flour
1 Tablespoon of Sugar
1 Tablespoon of Baking Powder
1 Tablespoon of Fresh Chopped Parsley
1/2 Cup of Milk
1/2 Cup of Buttermilk
1 Beaten Egg
1/2 Cup of Corn
1 Medium Onion

How to Prepare Your Cornbread

Fry the bacon and take out of the pan. Place the bacon grease in a measure and add oil to make 1/4 cup. Set aside. In a large bowl add the corn meal, flour, sugar, baking powder and parsley.

To this add the milk, buttermilk, egg and oil. Mix until all is combined. Add the bacon, crumbled, corn, and onion. Mix again.

Place in a greased 8 X 8 pan. Bake at 350 degrees for 45 minutes to an hour.

Thoughts, memories, recipes and notes:

_____

_____

_____

_____

_____

_____

_____

_____

_____

_____

_____

_____

_____

_____

_____

_____

_____

_____

_____

_____

_____

I See You

Milo loved mornings. He was so cuddly and warm and would just keep snuggling, trying to get as close as he could to you. He would watch your eyes so intently. If they moved even the slightest, he would start licking your lashes and then try to open your eyes by pulling on them. He would continue this as long as you kept them closed. But the minute you opened them, even just a little bit, in Milo's mind you were up and the day had begun!

Garlic Bagel Chips

These are so easy to make and they go great with split pea soup. You can make them as crunchy as you like and you can sprinkle them with just about any spice you wish.

Ingredients you will need

As Many Bagels As You Need Chips
Garlic Powder (Or Other Seasoning)
Salt
Pepper
Pam Cooking Spray

How to Prepare Your Chips

Slice the bagels very thin. Place on a cookie sheet and spray with Pam. Sprinkle the garlic powder (or any spice you wish) over them. Then salt and pepper.

Place in a 350 degree oven for about 15 minutes. But keep an eye on them; they can burn quickly.

Serve nice and warm with your bowl of soup.

Hot Greens

A nice portion of fresh greens, anything you have on hand. Beet greens, spinach or mustard. Anything you have a taste for.

Ingredients you will need

1/4 Pound of Bacon - Diced
Olive Oil
1 Small Onion - Chopped Coarse
1/2 Teaspoon of White Pepper
Juice of 1/2 Lemon
2 Garlic Cloves - Chopped
Hot Sauce - To Your Taste

How to Prepare Your Greens

Fry the bacon. Remove and to the bacon grease add a little olive oil (about 1 tablespoon) and sauté the onion and garlic until soft and tender. Chop up up the bacon and return to the pot. Add the fresh washed greens and cover. Cook down until tender and juice has all but evaporated. Usually about 20 minutes. Add the lemon juice and hot sauce.

Add the white pepper before serving.

These greens are excellent served with a little vinegar sprinkled on the top

Thoughts, memories, recipes and notes:

Time to Change

Milo was a people cat. It did not matter to him in the least if you did not like him. The minute you walked into our home, you were his. And I quarantee that by the time you left our home you were on your way to becoming a cat person. He was so affectionate and loving. He would jump on your lap or on the nearest table by you and begin his journey to transform you. If he didn't lick your hand, he would give you a hug. Believe me, Milo's hug melted more hearts than I can count. Anyone who walked into our house a dog person, left our house a cat person because of Milo. He just would not have it any other way.

The Bell

Milo loved to ring a bell that was hanging from the fireplace. He would do this at least once a day. Don't know why but he seemed to enjoy it. After Milo had left us, Tim and I were sitting on the couch thinking of our precious friend. Trooper was sitting between us. All of a sudden Trooper got up from the couch, walked over to the fireplace and rang the bell. He then came back over to us, put his face between us and just sighed. I guess Trooper missed his friend as much as we did.

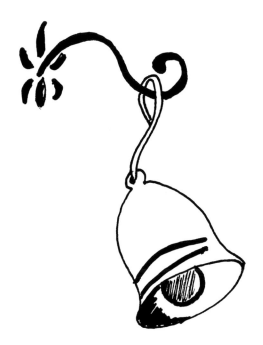

Just this side of Heaven is a place called Rainbow Bridge.

When a beloved pet dies, they go to Rainbow Bridge. There, there are meadows and hills for all of our special friends so they can run and play together. There is plenty of food and water and sunshine, and our friends are warm and comfortable. All the animals who had been ill or old are restored to health and vigor; those who were hurt or maimed are made whole and strong, just as we remembered them in our dreams of days and times gone by.

The animals are happy and content, except for one small thing; they miss someone very special to them, who had to be left behind.

They all run and play together, but the day comes when one suddenly stops and looks into the distance. The bright eyes are intent; the eager body quivers. Suddenly they begin to break away from the group, flying over green grass, their legs carrying them faster and faster. YOU have been spotted, and when you and your special friend finally meet, you cling together in joyous reunion, never to be parted again. The happy kisses rain upon your face; your hands once again caress the beloved head and you look once more into the trusting eyes of your pet, so long gone from your life but never absent from your heart.

THEN YOU CROSS RAINBOW BRIDGE TOGETHER . . . .

Tim and I hope we have brought a smile to your face with the happy times we have spent with Milo. If you have shed a little tear with the sad times, that's OK. In life you have to take the sad along with the happy. Milo was so very special to us. To this day we talk of him as if he were still with us. Then again, he will always be with us in our hearts.

This book is a small tribute to all that Milo has given to us.

Tim and I are giving 10% of the proceeds of Milo's book to various animal shelters. This way a little of Milo can be spread out to help small and large critters lead a better life.